Diminishing Resources

Soil

Diminishing Resources
Soil

Kevin Cunningham

MORGAN REYNOLDS
PUBLISHING

Greensboro, North Carolina

Diminishing Resources
SERIES

Soil | Forests | Water | Oil

Diminishing Resources: Soil

Library of Congress Cataloging-in-Publication Data

Cunningham, Kevin, 1966-
    Soil / by Kevin Cunningham.
        p.   cm. -- (Diminishing resources)
    Includes bibliographical references and index.
    ISBN 978-1-59935-114-8 (alk. paper)
  1. Soil conservation—Juvenile literature. 2. Soils—Juvenile
    literature. I. Title.
    S623.3.C86 2009
    333.73'16—dc22

2009010487

Printed in the United States of America
First Edition

Contents

Chapter One
Lessons of the Past

In the western Sudan, the region of Darfur ("the Land of the Fur," the Fur being one of the region's peoples) is being torn apart by a genocidal conflict between government-supported Arab herdsman and local African farmers. On the surface, the conflict appears strange. People on both sides are predominately Muslim, and the herdsmen and farmers lived for years in peace. The situation in Darfur is complicated and motivated by many issues, but a key component in the violent conflict is land. The herdsman and the farmers both desperately need the land—the soil—to survive and prosper, and there simply isn't enough to support all of those who need it. And making things worse, the amount of soil in the region is decreasing, rapidly.

The herdsman-farmer conflict is common throughout the world, and many believe the Sudanese government fed the tensions to assert control over the province. The Arab-dominated government, they say, favored Arab groups in clashes over dar and, as part of a program to modernize agriculture, took good land from African farmers and created huge mechanized farms.

According to human rights activist John Prendergast, "Climate change and the lack of rain are much less important than the land-use patterns promoted by the government . . . which were focused on intensive agricultural expansion that really mined the soils and left a lot of land unusable."

When farmers in Darfur rebelled against the proposed changes in land use, the Sudanese government armed militias like the *Janjaweed*, Arab horsemen blamed by human rights groups for atrocities across the province. What had simmered as a conflict over natural resources spun into a disaster that has included ferocious racial violence. The fighting threatened to carry over into neighboring Chad and to the large refugee camps in border areas. A conflict over land—and soil—may become a regional war.

Tragically, what is happening in Darfur—soil depletion leads to less food, which exacerbates pre-existing tensions leading to violence and war—is not an isolated case. Though it is often taken for granted, soil—land, dirt, ground—is an essential part of human civilization and survival, and when the soil a society needs is threatened, the consequences are disastrous.

Many of us tend to hold negative attitudes about soil, when we think about it at all. We don't want it on our shoes, in our houses, or billowing around us. The Old Norse expressed their own low opinion of the stuff by calling it *drit*, their word for excrement, and the origin of the English word dirt.

But soil is an essential natural resource, the stuff of life. It supports, directly or indirectly, every creature that lives on land, *Homo sapiens* included. The fertile, nutrient-rich topsoils capable of soaking up moisture and allowing air to circulate, like those in the American Great Plains, are a rare and difficult-to-renew resource. Humanity relies on between 8 and 11 percent of the world's soil to grow the entire food supply for more than 6 billion people. And the population keeps going up even as the amount of productive soil decreases.

While human beings have struggled with soil depletion since the first farmers tilled the ground, we have in recent times pushed much of our arable land to its limit. With increasing numbers of people to feed, and with huge profits to be made, farmers no longer let the land rest and replenish itself. The nutrients in the soil are often treated as a resource to be mined rather than a valuable inheritance to be maintained. Artificial fertilizers take the place of the complex system of organic matter, life, geological processes, and climate that created fertility in the first place.

The Earth's soil, the backbone of civilization for 10,000 years, is in danger of slipping through our fingers. Signs of a deepening problem include the loss of millions of acres to erosion and the spread of the world's deserts. The past offers examples of the price human beings have paid when the life-giving soil crumbles beneath them.

Soil depletion dates back to prehistory. Erosion—the movement of soil particles from the surface of the earth to someplace else through the action of rain and wind—began when the first Neolithic farmers churned up the ground with stone or wooden tools. From then on, flakes of soil have run off and blown away.

Humanity's growth and expansion in the wake of the agricultural revolution is a familiar story. Around 11,000 years ago, groups of Homo sapiens gradually abandoned a life that combined nomadic hunting (including fishing) and gathering for a settled life tending plants like wild rye and wheat. Growing crops and, later, herding livestock was a year-round commitment, with the payoff being a more reliable source of food and a supply of useful animal products. In time, food surpluses allowed a new kind of human society to arise, one capable of sustaining cities, culture, a nobility, religious and military castes, and trading systems.

The first great cities of the ancient world emerged in Sumer, in the fertile valley between the Euphrates and Tigris Rivers. As early as 3000 BC, 50,000 people lived in the city of Uruk.

But empires rise and fall, and Sumer was no different. While the causes of its decline were complex, Sumer failed in part due to environmental degradation and soil depletion in particular.

In the ancient world, as today, society runs at its most basic level by providing human necessities like food and clean water. Sumer's success encouraged a population boom. But the need to grow enough food to feed more and more people forced Sumerian farmers into destructive agricultural practices. Farmers could no longer allow land to lie fallow for a season or seasons so that the soil could reabsorb the nutrients and organic matter lost to previous crops. Uninterrupted plantings drained all the ground's stored-up nutrients. As a result, the soil produced less food over time.

The Sumerians also had a second soil problem. The soil in Sumer, like that in most semiarid regions, contained a high concentration of salt. When moisture evaporated from the ground, as it did in Sumer's ruthless summer heat, salt rose to the surface. Salt harms most human crops. Wheat, a Sumerian staple food, proved particularly vulnerable.

Widespread hunger caused by the problems with the soil contributed to unrest, and unrest to an era of political feuding that weakened the region's economy and military. After a period of decline, invasions by other groups finally ended Sumerian supremacy. Once-fertile Sumer became part of the Babylonian Empire.

The relationship between agriculture and other ancient civilizations worked in much the same way. On the one hand, rich soil and plentiful food provided a foundation for political stability, military might, wealth, culture, and population growth. On the other, those things attracted people, and more people required more food, and the pressure to fulfill that need eventually created problems.

Ancient Greece flowered into a dynamic civilization despite the fact only about 20 percent of the country had fertile land.

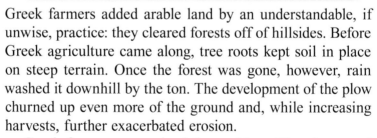

Ancient Agricultural Practices

Experts accept the once-radical idea of agricultural development taking place in regions independent of one-another. New research at a site along the Yangtze River suggests locals turned to growing rice during the same mini-Ice Age that inspired people at Abu Hureyra on the Euphrates River to try farming. Recent field work also suggests the Norte Chico region of Peru may have been the location of the only cities on Earth outside of Sumer and Egypt in 3200 BC. To the north, New World peoples in Mexico may have bred the scrawny teosinte plant into maize as early as 5100 BC. Even further off the beaten path, Papua New Guineans developed agriculture on their own, and pre-historic peoples in Egypt and India appear to have independently domesticated their own crops and livestock. ■

Greek farmers added arable land by an understandable, if unwise, practice: they cleared forests off of hillsides. Before Greek agriculture came along, tree roots kept soil in place on steep terrain. Once the forest was gone, however, rain washed it downhill by the ton. The development of the plow churned up even more of the ground and, while increasing harvests, further exacerbated erosion.

Greek farmers recognized the problem. They improved soil quality by stirring nutrients back into the ground, built terraces on hillsides to curb erosion, and allowed land to lie fallow. But by the time of Plato's birth in 427 BC, Greek cities imported at least a third of their food, perhaps much more. Plato wrote that the soil around Athens produced a fraction of what it had centuries earlier.

The Romans, like the Greeks, recognized the dangers of erosion and soil mining. Columella, author of a first-century treatise on farming, noted that his predecessors as well as his

The elements can hardly support us. Our wants increase and our demands are keener, while Nature cannot bear us.

Tertullian

peers had written about the increasingly unproductive farms around Rome. "We overcrowd the world," wrote Tertullian in the early third century. "The elements can hardly support us. Our wants increase and our demands are keener, while Nature cannot bear us."

Across the ocean, in the land that would become known as the Americas, agriculture played an equally vital role. Recent archaeology suggests people in the four river valleys of the Norte Chico, an otherwise arid area north of Lima, Peru, used irrigation to grow cotton and lived in cities as early as 3200 BC. Other peoples, from the mound builders in the Mississippi Valley to Central America's Olmecs to societies in the Amazon Basin, altered their landscapes for farming, and prospered by the decision.

Living in what is today Mexico, Belize, Honduras, and Guatemala, the Maya created the Western Hemisphere's first empire. Spreading out from the lowlands that nurtured farming must have required tremendous effort for people without metal tools or (except as toys) the wheel. But spread they did.

In AD 250, the Maya entered their so-called classic period of growth and accomplishment. As in other parts of the world, successful agriculture brought with it both the benefits of a dynamic culture and the stress of growing enough food to feed large numbers of people.

The soil itself presented special problems. Soil in tropical rain forests presents an odd contradiction. The ecosystems, with their thick, lush flora and dizzying variety of life-forms, would appear to enjoy super-fertile soil. In truth, tropical soils are nutrient-poor. Life thrives because rain forest ecosystems carry the great majority of available nutrients above, on, or

(continued on page 22)

Fuels for Soil

Tracing the flow of nitrogen shows how plants, animals, and soil work together. In nature, dead organic matter provides soil with nitrogen. Some microbes have evolved to turn nitrogen-rich matter into ammonium and nitrates, important nutrients used by plants. Less common but as valuable are bacteria known as rhizobia that live in the root systems of legumes, a family of plants that includes peas, beans, alfalfa, and clover. Rhizobia use a special enzyme to turn nitrogen gas—78 percent of our atmosphere—into ammonium that fuels the growth of the host plant. When the legumes die and decompose, the nitrogen they used returns to the soil for use by the next generation of plants. Scientists refer to this process as fixing nitrogen in the soil.

Removing the dead plants by cutting and harvesting takes the stored nitrogen out of the system, since very little of the nitrogen fixed by the rhizobia leaks into the surrounding soil. In order to replace the lost nitrogen, farmers must use fertilizers ranging from bird droppings to synthetic chemicals. ∎

Fertile Soil

The web of life in our soil is mostly unknown to scientists. A 2005 study from Los Alamos National Laboratory, using advanced DNA-detection techniques, claimed a single gram of good dirt was home to almost a million distinct species of bacteria. Estimates have placed about 10 trillion bacteria and acitonmycetes—veiny colonies of nitrogen-grabbing organisms—in one square meter of fertile, dry soil. Other important soil microbes include algae, with species that can soak up oxygen and others that help hold soil together; fungi; slow-to-grow lichens, able to dissolve rock with acids; and water-dwelling protozoa that prey on bacteria and provide food for animals further up the food chain. In addition, soil hosts masses of invertebrates—mites and springtails, worms and spiders, ants and termites—vital to the soil fertility. Vertebrates as varied as robins and badgers and prairie dogs, to say nothing of *Homo sapiens*, play a role, as well. ∎

near ground level. The forest canopy, for instance, steers rain down tree trunks and leaves, where it picks up valuable nutrients from animal excrement and decomposing organic matter. But plant roots spread horizontally through a shallow top layer—or even snake over the surface—and capture virtually all of the available nutrients before they reach the soil.

Honduras's Copán Valley was home to a successful Maya society. As was true across the Mayan world, its cities were man-made preserves for humanity in a sea of jungle and swamp. In 763, the young ruler Yax-Pac took power to find his 20,000 or more subjects straining the area's natural resources. The farmers, like in Sumer, kept planting their fields rather than letting the soil recharge. And, like the Greeks, they farmed easily eroded hillsides. Clearing the trees took away an important source of water and nutrients—there was no longer a canopy to direct rain or provide a home to animal life that provided organic matter. Erosion, meanwhile, made the hillsides unusable while simultaneously dumping nutrient-poor highland soil into lowland fields already degraded by overuse. Copán's nobility also wasted fertile land by putting up buildings on good soil.

Weather added another stress to the system. The Maya farmed in a climate with a distinct wet season followed by long months of drought. In years when the rains came late or failed to bring enough moisture, Mayan farmers, and by extension Mayan cities, faced hunger.

The archaeological record shows Copán's government deteriorated in the 820s. By then, cities throughout the southern Yucatan were dying out, often very quickly. Hunger wasn't the only problem—records suggest wars erupted across the entire region—but it aided in shaking the foundations of the societies. Over the next three hundred years, the Maya abandoned the Copán Valley's mined-out soils and eroded hillsides. By 1250, only a smattering of people remained. The rain forest reclaimed the cities and great pyramids. Mayan power and prosperity shifted north to cities like Chichén Itzá and Uxmal.

Environmental pressures weren't confined to empires, however. Island societies also struggled with the conflict between success and the toll it took on the soil.

One of the most striking things about Iceland's landscape is the absence of trees. Yet Viking relics and farm records, tests on pollen, and other sources make it clear that birch and willow forests once covered as much as 25 percent of the island.

That began to change in or around AD 874, when ships bearing Viking colonists and their Irish slaves made landfall. The colonists cleared the trees to build houses, create fields and pastures, and make the charcoal they needed to forge iron.

While Vikings have a reputation as the terrors of the medieval era, the Icelandic colonists actually had long experience as farmers in Norway and the British Isles. But Iceland's soil was new to them. The colonists' inability to adjust to its needs—indeed, their ignorance of the differences—would lead their society to the brink of collapse.

Iceland's soil renewed itself slowly, due to its fewer microorganisms and the shorter growing season at the island's high latitude. It also proved unusually prone to erosion. Iceland's soils are primarily andisols—one of the major components is volcanic ash supplied by the island's active volcanoes. Though ash adds nutrients to soil, it's extremely fine in texture. The ash in andisols could not—and did not—cohere into the kind of thick, erosion-resistant topsoil the Vikings had farmed farther south.

The natural plant cover had long protected the ground against erosion, both by deflecting water and rooting the soil in place. After settlement, however, rain and running water from snowmelt carried it away; the howling wind off the sea lifted it. In the last twelve centuries, as much as half of Iceland's original soil has washed away or blown into the Atlantic Ocean.

Nature also turned against the Icelanders. Around 1300, the climate throughout the Northern Hemisphere became colder and rainier. Harvests in Iceland, like those in continental Europe, fell off. Political and social pressures followed hunger, and Icelandic society entered a period of starvation, clan-based violence, and epidemics. Icelanders ultimately survived by adapting to the new circumstances, though not without drastic drop-offs in population and the standard of living.

As Adolf Fridriksson, head of the Icelandic Institute of Archaeology, said, "When you're living at the edge of the inhabitable world, any small change may have a huge effect. Especially if you're trying to live off nature, in isolation, as over here in Iceland."

It can be tempting to look at the ancient Maya or medieval Icelanders and dismiss their mistakes to ignorance. Farmers of earlier times lacked the scientific knowledge that informs agricultural decisions today. Yet even knowing what we know, some twenty-first century farmers and societies continue to repeat the mistakes of our ancestors—and to court hardship, starvation, and war.

Rapa Nui

Easter Island, or Rapa Nui, is the most remote island in the Pacific, a one-hundred-and-seventy square mile speck of land formed via volcanic activity. Polynesians arrived around AD 900 (scientific opinions differ on the date) and found an island covered in palm forests. The islanders' diet depended on sweet potatoes, and that staple food fueled a culture that created a writing system and its most famous works—stone platforms, called *ahu*, holding up the *moai*, great stone heads with impassive faces.

Rapa Nui's population grew until it peaked somewhere between a few thousand and perhaps 20,000 people. What happened next is part of a debate about how Rapa Nui's society imploded, why it might have happened, and what it could mean for the rest of us.

The best-known hypothesis about the islanders' fate states that those on Rapa Nui steadily exhausted the local natural resources, the soil included. Rapa Nui was a sensitive environment—dry, with a fine and fertile volcanic soil supporting palm forests, and an ecosystem with few native species. By 1600, and perhaps decades earlier, the islanders had stripped the landscape of trees. Erosion followed. Eventually, the lack of tree bark meant no more bark cloth for clothing, and the islanders, without wood to make canoes, could not get off Rapa Nui. Meanwhile, crops to feed the growing population exhausted the soil. Conflicts broke out over food resources. Starvation set in and the population crashed.

The people on Rapa Nui managed to arrest their decline short of extinction, but their culture never rebounded. European contact after 1722 opened up a grim era of disease and slavery. By 1872, the population had fallen to just one hundred-and-eleven Islanders. ∎

Chapter Two
Erosion

O ne of the worst erosion problems on earth is in one of the world's most fertile regions.

The Loess Plateau, located in China, is roughly as large as Belgium, the Netherlands, and France put together. It is named for a type of powdery silt—loess—that is a component in fertile soil not just on the plateau, but on the Great Plains of the United States.

For more than 2 million years, winds blowing off China's northwestern deserts dropped vast amounts of loess onto the plateau. So vast, in fact, that the fertile loess layer went hundreds of feet deep in some places. The loess nurtured forests, soon cleared by farmers moving into the region to create fields. The land's productivity, combined with access to the Yellow River, encouraged early Chinese civilization.

But loess's powdery grains made it very vulnerable to erosion. Mismanagement in the 1960s, encouraged by Chinese leader Mao Zedong, accelerated the devastation. Villagers carved terraces up and down the hillsides and planted crops. The short term gains in available farmland didn't last long. Rain washed out the terraces and carried away organic matter and nutrients. As harvests fell off, food became scarce. Farmers left in droves. Those staying behind fell into poverty. Some had to live in *yaodongs*, a kind of cave dug out of the loess, a traditional form of shelter used for thousands of years.

Today, erosion has carved parts of the plateau into semi-barren badlands. Other areas are brownish-gray deserts devoid

of almost all plant life. And the region still loses more than 1.5 billion tons of loess every year. Massive multi-ton chunks of soil collapse in mudslides during the summer rainy season or during earthquakes. A severe slide in 1983 destroyed four villages and killed more than two hundred people.

In 1994, the Chinese government and World Bank teamed to address the situation by starting a program aimed at stopping erosion and improving agricultural techniques. But experts agree the damage is so extensive that it will take generations to undo.

Erosion is a natural process. In fact, soil farmed today came into being in part because water and wind ground down surface rock over millions of years. Water erosion helped carve out the Grand Canyon, washed rich soil into valleys

between mountain ranges and down rivers into fertile lowlands like the Mississippi Delta.

Wind, the other erosive force, works by dislodging soil
and lifting it. As Iceland's early farmers learned, wind is particularly menacing to soil stripped of protective plant cover.
It affects different kinds of soil to varying degrees. Dry soil
and depleted soil, neither of which clumps together well, are
vulnerable. Wind velocities in an area also play a role, as
does the lay of the land; winds can generate greater force
howling over unbroken landscapes, as in northwest China,
than in forested areas.

Though often a destructive process, erosion under certain
circumstances benefits humanity. The Nile River carried
eroded fertile soil from Ethiopian hillsides via the river's

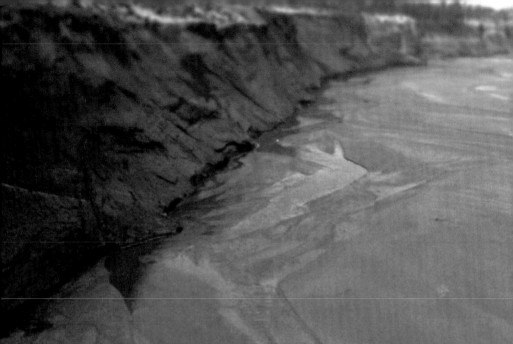

eastern branch, the Blue Nile. The White Nile flowing from the equatorial south brought humus—a dark, carbon-rich soil component heavy in decomposed plant matter. Rains upriver then brought floods to northern Egypt. As the waters receded, Egyptian farmers planted their crops in the rich silt and humus left behind. This annual replacement of nutrients allowed Egyptian farmers to produce crops year after year without exhausting their soil. Nature being nature, the system had limits. Sometimes the floods failed to arrive. But by and large the Nile fed a naturally productive agricultural region from the early days of history until Egypt's government dammed the river in the 1970s.

When people discuss erosion as a factor in soil depletion, they usually mean man-made erosion, sometimes referred to as accelerated erosion (technically, erosion in excess of what is caused by nature). Accelerated erosion overstresses a natural system. It's one of the most severe problems affecting soils, in part because the problem is so widespread, and in part because it often goes hand-in-hand with other soil depletion issues. In fact, all of the crises relating to soil in the new millennium can be blamed at least in part on erosion.

Simply put, the Earth is losing more soil to erosion than

can be replaced by man or nature.

Soil forms slowly. Once carried away by erosive forces, it takes at least two centuries for what's left behind to regenerate. And that's under ideal conditions. According to the U.S. Department of Agriculture, it takes five hundred years to create an inch of topsoil. In less-amenable soils, that inch may need a thousand years. And the period stretches into tens of thousands of years, and longer, for soils made up of coarse sand.

Accelerated erosion strikes hardest at the fertile layers nearest the surface. At the top lies the so-called "O horizon" made up of the autumn leaves, dead animals, fallen berries, spoiled pumpkins, and whatever other decomposing organic matter drops on the ground.

Beneath the O horizon is the "A horizon," or topsoil. For farmers, this is the richest part of the soil, the layer that under the best conditions sustains crops, gardens, forests, and other land-based plant life. Productive soil has an A horizon heavy with nutrients and decomposed organic matter. These factors work with microorganisms, soil gases, heat, and adequate water to nurture plant life, including what we grow for food.

Far less organic material sinks into the B horizon, or

subsoil. The clay-heavy matter found here keeps roots from growing and doesn't allow water or air to circulate. It also keeps both water and air from circulating. Below that is the "C Horizon," made up mostly of broken rock.

The depth of each soil horizon varies from place to place. Deserts often lack an O horizon, for example, and the A horizon may be thin or nonexistent in eroded areas. By contrast, untilled areas of the Great Plains have fertile A horizons many feet deep. But that's rare. Most topsoil is a foot deep or less.

Since the O horizon and A horizon hold most of a soil's nutrients, erosion inevitably impacts the health of a crop and the amount of it that can be harvested, called the yield. Low yields leave subsistence farmers and their families with less to eat. A farmer may find it harder to pay the rent, the mortgage, or taxes.

Left unchecked, erosion—like any environmental problem—can snowball, creating social problems or amplifying those that already exist, even threatening the survival of an entire society. While such scenarios are thought of as a thing of the past, there are countries in danger today of becoming failed states because of environmental collapse. One faces a grim fate because of erosion in particular.

In September of 2004, Tropical Storm Jeanne roared across Haiti. The heavy rains triggered floods called lavalas ("cleansing floods"). These rivers of reddish-brown mud swept away buildings, livestock, human beings—anything in the way—while choking off drainage canals and sewers. One lavala roared through the shantytowns ringing Port-au-Prince, the capital. Newspapers reported scenes of trucks dumping corpses into mass graves, of people lacking food or potable water clinging to rooftops. Estimates of the number of dead ranged from eight hundred to more than 2,000. Bodies of people and animals rotted in the open.

By contrast, the Dominican Republic, the other country on the island of Hispaniola, reported nineteen deaths. Experts pointed to the discrepancy in the death count as proof of the root cause of the disaster. The Dominican Republic has lush forests and ground covered with abundant plant life. Haiti, by contrast, is a brown and barren wasteland. And every storm washes more of its soil out to sea.

When Columbus landed on Hispaniola in 1492, he found a forested island inhabited by the Taino, an Arawak-speaking people. In time, the Spanish controlled the eastern part of Hispaniola while the French founded the colony of Saint Domingue in the more mountainous west. In order to grow sugarcane, tobacco, indigo, and other crops, the French cleared forest and brought in a massive slave labor force eventually numbering 700,000 people. Thanks to agriculture as well as valuable Haitian mahogany, Saint Domingue became France's most valuable overseas possession, the Pearl of the Antilles.

In 1804, a long-simmering slave revolt overthrew the French government. Society soon split between a French-speaking elite of landowners and the vast majority of Creole-speaking peasants. The elite kept the few fertile valleys. The peasants either worked for them or moved to marginal agricultural regions on mountainsides.

Today, Haiti is the Western Hemisphere's poorest country. All but a very few of its 8 million people work on tiny farms or have no job. On average, a Haitian woman lives to age fifty-four, a Haitian man to age fifty-two. Haiti's rate for human immunodeficiency virus (HIV) and AIDS is one the highest in the world outside Africa.

Of all the grim statistics, however, one stands out. The former Pearl of the Antilles has cut down all but 1 percent of its forests.

It was not always this way. As late as 1950, forest covered about a quarter of Haiti's land. Nor has the world ignored the problem. Governments and private groups have donated money, expertise, and even trees. Between 1997 and 2004, the U.S. Agency of International Development provided 4 million trees for farmers to plant, and tens of millions more in the years prior.

Haiti's modern battle with erosion began in the 1960s, the

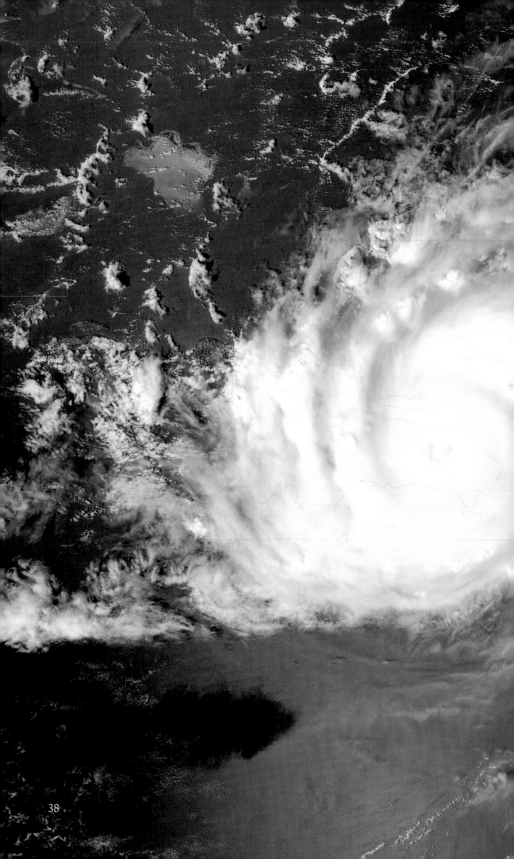

end of the country's era as an agricultural powerhouse. Falling coffee prices drove Haitian farmers to plant cash crops like peanuts and corn—crops that, unlike the coffee bush, need treeless land. Cutting down trees and planting corn on sloping land in Haiti had the same erosive effect as cutting down trees and planting wheat on the slopes of the Loess Plateau.

To add to the problem, the country fell under the rule of Francois "Papa Doc" Duvalier and his son Jean-Claude ("Baby Doc"), both of whom looted the country's natural resources for themselves and their supporters. During the two Duvalier eras (stretching from 1957 to 1986), the population of Port-au-Prince and other cities exploded as peasants, unable to make a living on farms, streamed in from the countryside in search of jobs. Jean-Claude's forced departure in 1986, while hailed as the end of a dictatorship, inaugurated a period of economic and political turmoil. A coup soon overthrew the democratically elected government. The world answered with a trade embargo. With other countries refusing to buy Haitian products, farmers lacked the cash to purchase seed and fertilizer. Seeing no choice, more and more of them gave up farming the land for life as *charbonniers* (charcoal-makers).

Charcoal is the product left over by heating wood in kilns or pits to create a carbon-rich fuel that resembles coal. Though a fuel-source usually associated with an earlier era in European or American history, charcoal still provides 85 percent of Haiti's energy. For many farmers, charcoal sells for much more than their crops. Faced with hunger and needing money, the charbonniers cut into the last stands of forest to sell the finished charcoal to urban businesses and households. As one farmer told a Florida newspaper, "We're not fools; we know that this is destroying the land, but charcoal is what keeps us alive."

The pursuit of charcoal creates interlocking vicious circles. Farmers sell it to the cities for fuel. But as the land degrades more people leave the country for the cities, increasing demand for charcoal. At the same time, deforestation aids erosion—one of the major reasons farms no longer produce enough to support rural people, and at the same a source of the lavalas that tear through the poor areas of cities inhabited by recent arrivals from the countryside.

As of 2009, two-thirds of Haiti's farmland is gone. Huge regions have lost not just the topsoil but the B horizon, exposing the infertile white bedrock. Rice production fell 30 percent in the 1990s. Haitians now grow less than 20 percent of this essential crop for themselves. Imported rice, meanwhile, recently doubled in price, putting it out of the reach of most Haitians. The poor have been forced to eat tree bark or pies made of clay mixed with salt and shortening. A great part of the $800 million Haiti receives in foreign aid every year is used just to hold off famine.

Erosion in Haiti comes close to a worst-case scenario for soil depletion, and is the current situation that best parallels the type of society-wide disaster that struck Rapa Nui. Foreign aid has at least spared Haiti that kind of total collapse.

Emigration to the U.S. and the Dominican Republic offers a way out to a small percentage of people while at the same time siphoning off part of the excess population. But neither is a long-term solution. How Haiti copes, and how the rest of the world helps it cope, may be a sign of how humanity faces the consequences of erosion, climate change, and other large-scale environmental issues in the coming decades.

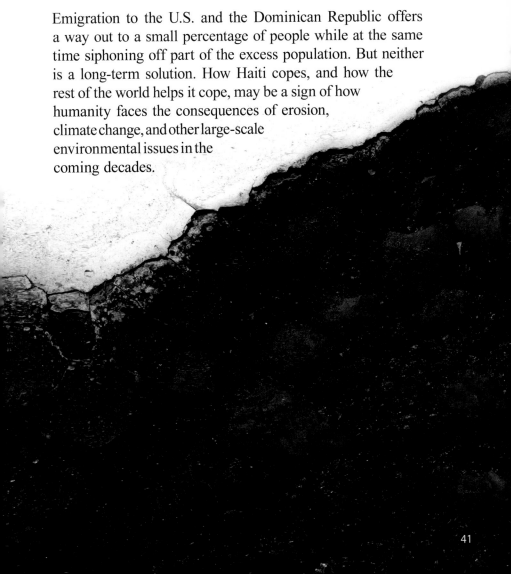

Combating Coastal Erosion

The effects of coastal erosion can cause serious problems. In many places, for example, oceanfront property sells for high prices. Waves and currents nibbling away at the shoreline bring the water so close to structures that the buildings must be abandoned.

In parts of Thailand, coastal areas lose up to five meters of land per year. Whole villages have had to move inland. The felling of Thailand's coastal mangrove forests makes the problem worse. Without thick mangrove roots to hold the soil, the shoreline erodes until chunks of it fall away. Thailand's mangroves have been felled to clear land for development, and for fish farms.

Development, dredging for shipping lanes, and hurricane damage has driven recent coastal erosion in the U.S. States up and down the coasts, as well as Hawaii and the Great Lakes states, have instituted programs to combat the problem. Recently, states have looked at the possibility of building living shorelines to replace bulkheads and seawalls that damage ecosystems and tend to crumble during hurricanes. In 2008, marine scientists in Mobile Bay, on Alabama's coast, sank a wall made of oyster shells. The idea is that sea life like oysters, fish, algae, and crabs will move into the oyster shell wall and create a natural barrier that can strengthen the shoreline, absorb waves, trap soil running off from the land, and, in time, reduce the shore's vulnerability. ■

Urban Erosion in Growing Communities

As suburbs and exurbs push further into rural areas, buildings and parking lots cover fertile soil. Soil experts see that in and of itself as a problem—a waste of a nonrenewable resource akin to Mayans building temples on good land. But development is also the major cause of urban erosion.

When a construction crew arrives on a site, one of the first things it does is level the land and strip away the vegetation. Building projects take time. During construction, the bare soil is left exposed to erosive wind and rain. Heavy machinery further aids the process by smashing it down. Compacted soil hardens and cannot absorb water. Since many building sites sit on high ground, the water runs off down the slope with enough speed to strip away even more soil at lower elevations.

The erosion threat doesn't end when the building is finished, either. Grassy lawns and popular landscaping plants lack the deep root systems that anchor soil in place. Rainwater gushing from a gutter can gouge a trench in a lawn. Water runoff forms rivulets beside pavement and sidewalks.

Wherever water runs downhill, it carries a sludge of soil and other particles called sentiment. In urban areas, sentiment runs into sewers and drainage tunnels. That system usually leads to nearby rivers or other waterways.

Sentiment contamination is a leading cause of pollution in streams, but it also affects the environment in other ways. For example, sentiment buries animal and plant habitats, stunts plant growth, can make it harder for fish species to find food, and harms fish and insects. Since sentiment-heavy water absorbs solar heat, the water becomes warmer, and native species may fail to thrive in the new temperatures. ■

Chapter Three
Exhaustion

U sing land for agriculture depletes the soil of nutrients. Unless managed properly, soil in even fertile regions loses the ability to sustain crops. Soil scientists call the practice soil mining—extracting nutrients from the soil the same way we extract gold, uranium, or limestone. Soil mining is a major cause of soil depletion, and contributes to hunger and poverty.

Soil mining takes place on every continent. The practice is harmful in and of itself, both to the land and in the long term to the people who rely on it. But, like erosion, it also works hand-in-hand with other factors to deplete the soil. Some factors, like rainfall and temperatures, are literally forces of nature. Others come about because of agricultural practices and leaving the ground bare, for instance. While causes vary, the result is that crops refuse to grow. Disaster often follows.

Before 1930, the Great Plains had known decades of amazing fertility. For sixty years, people had flocked there to make a living from farming, drawn by the lure of cheap land and promises of soil so rich it could grow anything in great abundance.

The claims got outrageous at times, but the Plains did in fact have some of the most fertile land on earth. During the Ice Age, glaciers chewed up North American soil that winds then dropped on the Plains and the Midwest. Deep-rooted prairie grasses kept the soil in place. Over thousands of years, dead plants added layers of nutrients and organic matter. Herds of bison even fertilized the ground. As a result, the topsoil was deep and rich, and it held rainwater as well as any farmer could ask.

After 1900, mechanical equipment allowed farmers to till more and more land. The World War I years encouraged even greater production as the government bought up wheat and sent prices soaring. Farmers, sensing a huge payday, churned up millions of acres of virgin grassland to plant as much wheat as possible.

Prosperity didn't last, however. A postwar fall in prices drove many farmers into debt and off the land. Those able to survive the economic crunch needed to plant more crops on more land to stay afloat. Manufacturers like John Deere and International Harvester complied by building even larger farm machinery. The new generation of equipment allowed farmers to work more ground faster, but pulverized the topsoil. Parts of the Plains, a region of high winds and violent rainstorms, began to erode.

Then it quit raining. Drought transformed the once-fertile Great Plains into a wasteland called the Dust Bowl.

The climate on the Plains has always cycled between wet and dry periods. As the 1930s began, a sixty-year era of reliable rainfall came to an end. Drought and tremendous summer heat blasted a large portion of the 1931 wheat crop. The soil, barren of cover and chewed up by decades of farming, turned gray and dry and as hard as concrete.

For ten years, the United States witnessed terrifying spectacles of wind-blown erosion. Dust storms thousands of feet high blown by hundred-mile-per-hour winds pounded the plains. On April 14, 1935, a series of "black blizzards" plunged cities into total darkness at midday.

When a storm came, farmers and their families fled into cellars, and later emerged to find dust piled as high as the windows of their houses. Caroline Henderson, the wife of a farmer, wrote:

Any attempt to explain the violent discomfort of these storms is likely to be vain except to those who have already experienced them. There are days when for hours at a time we cannot see the windmill fifty feet from the kitchen door. There are days when for briefer periods

one cannot distinguish the windows from a solid wall because of the solid blackness of the raging storm. . . . This wind-driven dust, fine as the finest flour, penetrates wherever air can go. . . . A friend writes of attending a dinner where "the guests were given wet towels to spread over their faces so they could breathe." . . . . "Dust to eat" and dust to breathe and dust to drink. Dust in the beds and in the flour bin, on dishes and walls and windows, in hair and eyes and ears and teeth and throats, to say nothing of the heaped up accumulation on floors and window sills . . .

Storms dumped Plains' soil on New York City and Washington, D.C. Ships two hundred miles out in the Atlantic saw brown clouds of dirt whipping off the eastern seaboard. Even on days when the wind didn't blow, hardships piled up for local farmers. The ongoing drought destroyed crop after crop. In 1935, a freak swarm of starving jackrabbits descended on farmland, eating what little had grown. "Dust pneumonia," caused by inhaling grit, killed people up and down the Plains—doctors reported corpses with lungs full of dirt.

People fled the Plains, more than 3 million in all. The general economic hardship of the Great Depression added to the

(continued on page 54)

"We Americans have been the greatest destroyers of land of any race or people barbaric or civilized."

Hugh Bennett

misery. Many found it difficult to find other jobs, ending up hungry and homeless, constantly migrating in search of work.

Hugh Bennett, head of the government's Soil Erosion Service and a longtime critic of Plains farming practices, said, "We Americans have been the greatest destroyers of land of any race or people barbaric or civilized."

The U.S. government under President Franklin Roosevelt launched a number of programs to fight the disaster. Experts encouraged farmers to plant several different crops, rather than just wheat, as a hedge against exhausting the soil. The Roosevelt government, despite criticism and even mockery, also encouraged shelterbelts—lines of trees—to slow the winds. The government planted close to 220 million trees from North Dakota to Texas. Though the rain and better times returned, the Great Plains never recovered its former population. Giant corporate farms rather than family farms dominate the region today.

The Dust Bowl raised awareness of the relationship between agriculture and soil depletion. But the planet is losing huge amounts of soil–1 percent of the world's topsoil each year, experts say. Agriculture is the biggest culprit. A 2006 Cornell University study claimed the U.S. loses soil ten times faster than nature can replenish it. The figure rises to at least 30 percent in China and India. Estimates of what this costs vary, but the Cornell study said the U.S. pays about $37.6 billion per year in lost productivity.

The U.S. still has problems when it comes to soil loss. Perhaps less in the news than soil issues elsewhere—no Haiti-level catastrophes, and no chance of starvation, one of the grim side-effects in Africa—but it exists. Given the country's huge agriculture industry, the amounts of soil lost add up to big numbers.

Washington state's Palouse Hills, for example, is a major wheat-growing center, a land of fertile loess soil. By 1950, 80 percent of the land had lost somewhere between a fourth and three-fourths of its topsoil, with another 10 percent hav-

ing lost it all. The average acre lost nine tons of soil every year. Land on sloping hills lost far more. Eroded furrows called rills criss-crossed once-fertile areas; dust storms were a problem; one farmer noted that he switched to soil-friendly methods simply because every spring water running off the hills dropped a foot of mud—eroded soil—around his house. Even with some farmers adopting soil conservation strategies, however, the Palouse soil remains seriously degraded, and untold tons of it is lost. Farmers now use fertilizers to maintain productivity.

The same is true, in fact, throughout much of the U.S. American farmers use more than 20 million tons of fertilizer on their crops. The excess drains into river basins, especially in the spring, the wettest time of year in agricultural regions. Large rivers like the Missouri and Ohio, as well as an enormous tributary system, carry soil and fertilizer runoff from thirty-one states into the Mississippi River. As the Mississippi leaves the state of Louisiana, it spits dirt choked with fertilizer into the Gulf of Mexico.

The nitrogen products in fertilizer helps plants grow. *Any* plants, including the algae native to the gulf. Algae growth throughout the spring and early summer leads to a massive die-off. At the same time, microscopic zooplankton feeds on the algae and excretes part of it as waste. As all this plant matter decomposes, the water becomes hypoxic—starved of oxygen—in the lower- and middle depths.

Sea life needs oxygen as much as humans do. When a hypoxic event blooms into a massive dead zone, it suffocates any animal unable to flee. Along the Louisiana and Texas coasts, this includes shrimp and other food species vital to the fishing economy.

From 2000 to 2007, dead zones close to or above 8,000 square miles in size—an area roughly equal to Delaware and Connecticut together, stretching from the southern tip of Louisiana west along the coastline as far as west as Galveston,

Texas—appeared in three different summers. The dead zone exceeded 8,000 square miles again in 2008.

And it's possible the problem will worsen. As global food prices have climbed in recent years, U.S. farmers and agribusiness companies have planted more crops and used more fertilizer in order to boost profits.

Australia is also facing a farming-related environmental crisis, one caused in great part by a practice as ancient as Sumer: irrigation. Australia's soil is old and worn out. Processes that renewed soil elsewhere played little part in the continent's geology. For example, volcanic ash enriched the

soil in Iceland and Hawaii, but volcanoes haven't existed on most of Australia for one a hundred million years. The glaciers that chewed rock into loess for the Great Plains never reached beyond the southern tip of the island continent, and geologic processes that brought fertile soil to the surface in parts of Europe and India only occurred rarely in Australia.

It looked fertile enough at first glance, however. When European colonists arrived, they found abundant forests and grasslands along the coasts. Crops went in, sheep were sent out to graze. The relatively poor soil received nutrients from fertilizers, and Australia grew into one of the world's great producers of wheat and wool.

But Australia's coastal climate turned out to be unpredictable. Only the southwestern region gets reliable rain. As a result, much of the country's agriculture depends on irrigation.

A great deal of Australia's soil is salt-heavy, a legacy of winds blowing sea salt off the surrounding oceans and of a time when salt water seas covered parts of the continent. Irrigation saturates the soil. The moisture sinks through the topsoil to the layer of salt farther underground. Water provides a medium for salt to rise toward the surface. (Alternately, the salt may sink into groundwater and find its way to the surface via streams and rivers.) After years of irrigation, the salt deposits have begun to contaminate Australia's soil, a condition known as salinization, or excessive salt in the soil.

A related problem, dry land salinization, is related to the loss of ground cover. Plants with deep roots—and some wild

prairie grasses have root systems twenty-feet long—absorb enough water to keep the excess from reaching the salt layer. Farming, however, focuses on short-lived plants with relatively shallow root systems. Furthermore, the crops only grow on the soil part of the year. The rest of the time the ground is bare and rainwater penetrates deeper. The groundwater, now laden with salt, rises. The water evaporates or is used by plants, but the salt remains behind, often as a white crust on the land.

Salt can be found in soil in many places, but usually in such small amounts that it doesn't affect plant life. Increase

salinity, however, and many plants, including almost all those grown for food, fail to thrive or simply die. Some call it the white death, because of the color of salt-heavy ground.

In Australia, salinization affects almost 10 percent of the country's land. This is an ominous number considering that salt-sensitive wheat is the country's leading export crop, and that the fabled Wheat Belt in the country's southwestern corner is one of the areas under the most intense pressure.

According to the Australian government, salinization costs the country's agriculture sector more than $130 million every year. But that's only part of the cost. High concentrations of salt in the water can ruin fields downstream. Furthermore, the salt flowing into Australia's river system eats away at roads, bridges, building foundations, pipes, cables, and other infrastructure. City dwellers in southern Australia have learned to watch for salt collecting on bricks and pavement—signs of salt concentration that can damage property, lawns, and gardens.

The same rivers provide the water for the majority of Australia's population. Several Australian cities rely on the Murray-Darling River system. But salinity threatens to make the water too salty for safe human consumption.

Whatever the environmental problems related to agriculture, fertilizers and irrigation are important tools, and it is unlikely farmers will give up either in the near future, not with so much of their crop yield depending on those tools, and not with so much of the world's population depending

on the yield. Long-term change will require shifts in farming methods and priorities, in government policy, and in public attitudes. Consumers, after all, demand low prices for food, and low prices depend on the kind of huge supplies made possible by high yields; while at the same time any increase in food prices in the developing world would literally be the difference between life and death for millions of people.

The lessons of the past, as well as those of the present, may point the way to progress against soil problems, may even lead to solutions. The question is if we'll make the decisions necessary before the numbers catch up to us. Right now, we lose 1 percent of the soil per year. What happens when that adds up to 20 percent, or 50, or more?

The Wheat Fields of Kazakhstan

In the 1950s, the then-Soviet Union decided to turn the so-called virgin lands of Kazakhstan into wheat fields. Farmers planted on more than a hundred million acres of unbroken or abandoned soil—a great deal of it marginal. At first it seemed to work. A bumper wheat crop in 1956 promised great things. But the virgin lands project soon became a fiasco. Farmers left the land bare during fallow periods. Huge amounts of soil, stripped of grass cover, blew and washed away. The Soviet government added to the problem by insisting much of the land be used solely for wheat. That kind of monoculture (one-crop) farming virtually guarantees soil exhaustion because repeated sowings of the same plant suck up the specific nutrients needed by that crop. As a result, the soil was exhausted by the mid-1960s.

Short-sighted planning, along with drought and mismanagement, undercut later harvests, and soon the Soviets had to import Canadian grain. Today, Kazakhstan's farmers grow about one-eighth the amount of wheat as a farmer in France with the same amount of land. ■

Rabbits and Sheep Down Under

Australians continue to clear native plants in order to turn land into pasture. But animals contribute to the damage, too. Sheep in Australia, as in Iceland a thousand years ago, eat down the plant life before it can grow back.

But sheep aren't the only animal responsible. Australia's soil erosion can also be traced in part to the world's most

infamous rabbit problem. Introduced during the early days of settlement, the European rabbit bred wildly in Australia thanks to a lack of native predators. The booming rabbit population ate everything—crops, trees, bushes—and their collective appetite not only wiped out native plants, but starved the native animals that ate those plants. In the 1950s and again in the 1990s, the government introduced diseases to thin the rabbit population. But despite the millions of dead rabbits, the animal remains a serious pest. ∎

When Levees Break

Soil does more than grow food. In New Orleans, located at or below sea level, it provides protection in the form of earthen walls, called levees. At least, it's supposed to.

In some places, clay-heavy soils provided the main building material; other sections relied on sandy soils. With Katrina's arrival, waves of water crashed over the levees. The motion of the waves and water, called "scour" by engineers, eroded the soil on the earthen levees, causing instability and even collapses. Clay levees, capable of handling the water, managed to stand up better than sand, but enough of the system gave way to allow catastrophic floods in large parts of the city.

After Katrina, the Army Corps of Engineers studied new ways of preventing scour and other factors that contributed to the disaster. In addition to raising and widening levees, the Corps of Engineers chose to *armor* levees. As the name suggests, armoring protects a levee from the kind of fierce water erosion kicked up by hurricanes. Armoring, as it turns out, has a lot in common with restoring eroded hillsides or plains. The Corps of Engineers planted grass on levees as a soil anchor and to deflect water. In other places, concrete slabs or stone grouted in place serve a similar purpose. Armoring efforts have concentrated especially on places where levees contain existing water sources like Lake Borgne, located to the city's east.

The levee system rehab is not due to be finished until 2011, and the Corps of Engineers has faced criticism of its methods. For example, in 2007, engineering professor Robert G. Bea released an independent study pointing to deep furrows caused by erosion along one levee near Lake Borgne.

The Corps' chief in New Orleans noted, however, that plans called to top porous, vulnerable soils with stronger clay soils better suited to resist erosion. In one article, Bea said, "It's like icing on the top of angel food cake. These levees will not be here if you put a Katrina surge against them."

In the summer of 2008, the new levee system passed its first test: the storm surge from Hurricane Gustav. But Gustav was a weaker storm than Katrina. Whether the system can resist a stronger storm remains to be seen. ∎

Chapter Four
Desertification

The United Nations defines about 40 percent of the world's land as dry land. Dry lands by definition lose substantially more water through evaporation than they receive via rainfall and include arid regions (such as sandy deserts like the Sahara), as well as semiarid and dry subhumid areas. The lack of moisture, combined with overall poor soil quality, make dry lands vulnerable to desertification.

Desertification has nothing to do with the actual spread of deserts (though it can seem this way, since dry lands often border deserts). Instead, it refers to a process that transforms fertile or marginally fertile areas into wastelands incapable of supporting agriculture. A lack of rainfall is only part of the story. The range of human activities that damage the soil—erosion, deforestation, overgrazing, and soil mining—contribute as well.

It happens everywhere. Desertification has overwhelmed huge parts of the Loess Plateau. It has turned part of Iceland into Europe's largest sandy desert and is blasting the once-fertile areas of Kazakhstan around the Aral Sea. Desertification is one of the key causes of the soil depletion currently happening in the Darfur region, spurring on the conflicts there. The human costs of desertification can be enormous. As the

United Nations Convention to Combat Desertification puts it:

> *Desertification exacerbates poverty and political instability. It contributes significantly to water scarcity, famine, the internal displacement of people, migration, and social breakdown. This is a recipe for political instability, for tensions between neighboring countries, and even for armed conflict. Evidence is mounting that there is often a strong correlation between civil strife and conflict on the one hand and environmental factors such as desertification on the other.*

That evidence, like desert sand, has piled up for more than thirty years in the region of Africa known as the Sahel.

Sahel comes from the Arabic word *sahil*, meaning "shore of the desert." Stretching from the Atlantic coasts of Senegal and Mauritania to Ethiopia on the India Ocean, the Sahel marks a transitional belt between the Sahara Desert and the more fertile equatorial zone that dominates the central part of Africa.

On average, six inches of rain falls along the Sahel's northern edge, though this varies year to year and place to place. Four times as much (again with variances) falls on the southern edge. Thus, a traveler moving south to north across the Sahel would encounter steadily diminishing rains. Here and there lush areas thrive, fed by localized rainfall and collection points at lakes and watering holes. In these places, plant life remains diverse and healthy, and the exotic animal life in the region includes gazelles and rare species of antelope. But these islands of life are only an echo of a Sahel that, even fifty years ago, supported ecosystems inhabited by ostriches, giraffes, lions, and forest-dwelling monkeys.

Traveling north, hardscrabble subsistence farms give way to grassland, and grassland to a semiarid region where clumps of sparse vegetation jut up from the sandy soil. The only tall plants are a few lonely trees, spread far apart. In time, all but the hardiest vegetation gives way to the sand and rocks of the Sahara.

The region has been home to farmers and nomadic herders for thousands of years. Traditionally, the farmers kept land fallow for long periods to allow the soil to regenerate. At the same time, the nomads' cattle and sheep herds, passing this way and that in search of grass, ate the leftover plant waste off the farmers' fields while providing fertilizer for the next crop.

Changing agricultural policies imposed by European colonial governments disrupted the age-old system, first by limiting where nomads could drive their herds, and second by forcing local farmers onto ever-more marginal land to free up the best soil for plantations that grew peanuts, cotton, and other profitable crops. As the subsistence farmers stressed their less-fertile land, the herders gathered larger numbers of animals for profit and to pay steep colonial taxes.

These changes brought about the usual consequences. Crops failed in the increasingly weary soil. Wind and rain then went to work on the exposed fields, further depleting fertility. Herders, meanwhile, drove their flocks onto land lacking adequate food, and monopolized water springs and wells. The constant presence of livestock degraded the nearby land and cut off wildlife from valuable water sources.

Despite the problems, the Sahel's population boomed. Three times as many people lived there in 1970 as in 1930. Livestock numbers rose, as well. Both figures continued to increase as European nations gave up their claims. Sudan became independent from Great Britain in 1956, Guinea-Bissau from Portugal in 1973. Other than never-colonized Ethiopia, the other nations touched by the Sahel achieved independence between those two dates.

A dry period set in as the 1960s came to a close. Drought struck hard, but the situation worsened in 1972, when vir-

tually no rain fell. Crops and grass in the marginal lands refused to grow. Worse, the plant matter left over from the previous year had been devoured by livestock herds. The West African countries of the region had few agricultural or financial resources to weather drought. What existed they put into the peanuts and cotton sent abroad for much-needed cash.

As the drought worsened, somewhere between 100,000 and 250,000 people died of starvation. Photos circulated world-wide showing emaciated children and a barren landscape strewn with the corpses of dead livestock. It was just the beginning. Drought hammered parts of the Sahel until 1984.

The change in the weather, however, wasn't new or even unusual. The Sahel had endured periodic dry periods for

thousands of years. At any rate, rainfall isn't the driving force behind desertification. The semiarid lands ringing deserts are naturally dry (thus semiarid), yet in the past had supported diverse plant and animal life, despite drought cycles.

What changed was the fact that the Sahel had to support more intensive agriculture and far greater human populations. When the 1972 drought hit, the increased numbers of humans and livestock had used up the soil nutrients and organic matter as well as food and water. Little or nothing remained to tide people over through the hard times, unlike in the past, when relatively few human beings lived off the Sahel's vulnerable land.

The Sahel's boundaries have shifted southward since the 1960s. The desert has followed. Dunes have crawled into the outskirts of Nouakchott, the capital of Mauritania. Without careful management and fertilizers to revive the soil—and both are expensive—desertification and its consequences may get even worse, and because the human population keeps growing, the people have no choice but to mine the soil of its remaining fertility just to stay alive.

And that choice is an important part of the problem. Desertification hits hard at poor regions in part because people are desperate. The people of the Sahel, like Haiti's *charbonniers*, may recognize the long-term damage they're doing, but first and foremost they want to survive. Under those circumstances, conservation takes a back seat.

The Sahel's situation contrasts with activities in a far more affluent part of the world north of the Sahara. In Spain, it is questionable human decisions, along with climate change, that have raised the risk of desertification.

The province of Murcia sits on the country's southeastern coast. Semiarid in climate, Murcia is often battered by one-hundred-degree temperatures during the summer. But in recent years tourists seeking Murcia's bright sunshine have encouraged a boom in golf courses and vacation resorts. At the same time, some of Murcia's farmers, taking advantage of new irrigation opportunities, have invested in profitable water-hungry crops.

To sustain these changes, Murcia uses more than twice as much water from the system than goes in. Developers and farmers have drilled thousands of illegal wells, trade fresh water on a booming black market, and fight one-another for

the rights to the legal water overseen by the government. Locals have resorted to all kinds of tricks to increase how much they receive, including bribery and declaring the grass on golf courses to be a "crop." As a result, the water supply is drying up.

This comes at a time when statistics suggest temperatures are rising in Murcia— and the rest of Spain. The *New York*

Times reported a 2.7 degree rise in surface temperatures since 1880, almost double the global average of 1.4 degrees. With overgrazing and irrigation serious problems throughout the country, the government declared 37 percent of Spain at risk for desertification, with Murcia among the provinces in the most danger.

The situation in Spain may be pointing to a bigger problem. The frequency of droughts since the year 2000, to say nothing of record high temperatures and melting polar ice, may be signs we're already seeing consequences of climate change today.

But while most scientists agree climate change is happening, judging its effects on specific places is often difficult due to the complexity of natural systems like weather, and because a lot of research has yet to be done. How much climate change is fueling, say, desertification in the Sahel, is part of an ongoing scientific debate. New research doesn't absolve climate change as a cause, but it does suggest that blaming it for the Sahel droughts is too simple.

Changes in the atmosphere and the oceans may have played a more dramatic role in Sahelian weather than previously realized. Since the 1980s, scientists have modeled the region's climate on sophisticated computer programs. Some models suggest the surface temperatures of the oceans on either side of Africa—the Atlantic to the west, the Indian to the east—have changed. The changes have in turn altered the pattern of the annual rains. While certain research claims the Atlantic's temperature plays the dominant role, other research points to changes in the Indian Ocean.

The uncertainty of the science makes it difficult to foresee the Sahel's future. In 2005, for instance, two American researchers predicted increased rainfall caused by climate change. But later that year a team at the U.S. National Oceanic Atmospheric Administration said the exact opposite: "[Our] model projects a drier Sahel in the future, due primarily to increasing greenhouse gases." Still others suggest that climate change will cause the Sahel's rains to become more unpredictable.

In the meantime, the dry lands become deserts. Drought-related forest fires and desertification menace the Canary Islands. The Gobi threatens to overwhelm parts of the Loess Plateau, while farther west overgrazing has drawn the Kumtag Desert to the outskirts of Dunhuang, an ancient city and home to 100,000 people. Mali's Lake Faguibine, a lifeline for more than 200,000 people, has gone dry in just the last generation, depleted by the Sahel drought, its feeder canals overwhelmed by sand.

And it will take more than rain to solve the problem

Sahel Renewed

Since the early 1990s, an increase in rainfall has allowed a substantial part of the Sahel to become green again. Wild and cultivated vegetation in parts of Chad, Mali, and Mauritania covers 50 percent more land than during the drought years, and studies made on the ground and with satellite imaging show increases in ground cover beyond what can be explained by the rainfall. Irrigation explains some of the change. A renewed commitment to soil improvement and water conservation—often using traditional methods used by people in the region in the past—have also contributed. ∎

Chapter Five
Rebuilding the Soil

Tackling the problems that contribute to soil depletion will require an effort on many fronts. First and foremost, people must address the way soil is used for agriculture. At the same time, the problem-solving has to take into account that different nations have different capabilities—economic, educational, and otherwise—and that even within one country, soil types vary dramatically, with each soil affected by a host of factors, and with a different solution required for specific situations.

Few of those studying the problem doubt that those solutions are needed, and sooner rather than later. "Growing large amounts of crops in a way that decreases our ability to do so in the future invites disaster," said David Montgomery, a professor of geomorphology at the University of Washington.

The core of what people like Montgomery suggest is a number of practices—in many ways a revised method of agriculture—that falls under the heading sustainable farming. This catch-all term refers to agricultural practices that encourage crop production while also making the maintenance of healthy soil a priority.

A number of sustainable strategies are already being tried. Some U.S. farmers, for example, have taken an interest in cutting their use of artificial fertilizers. This is in part because of soil problems. The price of petroleum, however, has also had an impact. Because many fertilizers (and pesticides) are mixed with petroleum products, the recent rise in petroleum prices—from $23 per barrel in 2001 to more than $140 barrel in mid-2008—has increased the cost of fertilizing crops. Though no one expects farmers to give up using fertilizer, easing back on its use may become necessary to maintain a farm's bottom line.

The fertilizer issue shows in a nutshell the relationship between profits and any proposed change in agriculture methods. In the end, financial considerations will guide the adoption of any sustainable farming practice. A family farm is a business, after all, and if a farmer fails to make money, he'll lose his farm, his job, and a substantial investment. The corporate mega-farms that dominate U.S. agriculture put even more of a premium on profit. So if a reform causes a decline in yields, if it raises the cost of growing a crop, if it asks for too radical a change, it's likely farmers and agri-business would pass on implementing it, regardless of any positive impact on soil depletion.

Governments and advocates for sustainable farming have also addressed problems related to irrigation, in particular erosion and salinization. In Australia, dry land salinity spurred the creation of a monitoring system that uses data from airplanes and satellites to identify areas vulnerable to salinization.

Another mostly desert nation, Israel, has attacked its salinity problem by breeding salt-resistant fruit and vegetable crops. The country's farmers also use drip irrigation in its dry lands. Drip irrigation employs a system of drippers, sprayers, or lines under plant roots to directly introduce moisture to plants. As a result, the ground can absorb the water,

eliminating the evaporation that draws salt to the surface. In addition, Israeli farmers can use wastewater or brackish water pumped from under the desert rather than dip into its limited supply of fresh water. And there are other advantages. Drip irrigation reduces the amount of fertilizer and other chemicals leached from the ground as well as drastically cutting erosion.

The drawbacks are considerable, however. Installing a drip irrigation system—with its interconnected pumps, tubes, filters, valves, and drippers/sprayers—requires a significant amount of money. Some components are vulnerable to harsh desert weather. Ease of use can be an issue, as well. Rolling up drip irrigation machinery for the off-season takes time and any large-scale system must be adapted to a farm's unique landscape and soil.

Another sustainable practice takes a new approach to the ancient task of plowing the land for planting. Plowing damages the soil over time. Open ground becomes vulnerable to erosion, and the process disrupts the ecosystem in the upper layers while at the same time chopping up and exposing organic plant matter that otherwise would add nutrients.

But an increasingly popular alternative, no-till farming, eschews turning over the soil in the spring. The farmer instead leave fields covered with crop residue—the leftover plant matter from previous crops—and uses disking to return some of this organic material to the soil. When it's time to plant, specialized seed drills are used to drive seeds through the organic layer. The layer protects and warms the seedling while the soil itself, protected by residue from wind and rain,

is less vulnerable to erosion. In fact, in some places, no-till farming has cut erosion between 75 and 90 percent.

One other benefit: the crop residue keeps soil moist and warm through the winter, a favor to earthworms and other organisms that contribute to fertility.

As always in agriculture, no method works well everywhere. Many factors figure into erosion rates, for example, so not every farm benefits equally. And clay-heavy soils resist no-till's benefits, because without tilling the ground can become compacted—smashed down into a hard, cement-like layer. Tradition prevents many farmers from embracing no-till. So does the cost, as no-till fields often require more pesticides and herbicides. While the improved soil quality offsets some of the need for chemicals in later years, not all farms have the desire or the ability to make the initial investment.

The disadvantages aside, no-till and leaving crop residue have caught on in North America. In Canada, the percentage of farms using these methods rose from 33 percent to 60 percent between 1991 and 2001. While American farmers have been slower to adopt no-till, it was practiced on more than 20 percent of U.S. farmland in 2004. And the number

is on the rise, in part because of a financial incentive—plowing takes fuel, and plowing less saves money.

A discovery in the Amazon inspired another, more experimental proposal to reinvigorate the soil—while at the same time providing a possible tool for helping with soil depletion and climate change.

In recent years, archaeological work led by the late American archaeologist James Petersen, Brazilian archaeologist Eduardo Neves, and American anthropologist Michael Heckenberger unearthed evidence that, prior to European contact, Amazonian peoples used irrigation and managed their soil for agriculture. Since these civilizations used wood for buildings, little evidence of the people remained above ground into the modern era.

But the ground itself told an epic story. Starting perhaps 2,300 years ago, societies in the Amazonian Basin began to engineer their environment to accommodate agriculture. At the Hatahara site in Brazil, Neves' team found that farmers had come to the area at least four separate times. They appeared to have lived on a diet of fish, wild meat, fruits, and manioc, and cleared trees for farming with tools and fire. But the fires burned slowly so that, instead of consuming the trees, it turned them into carbon-rich charcoal and soot—a product called biochar (or char). The process, called slash-and-char, locks up a tree's nutrients. Two found in biochar, potassium and phosphorus, are important to plant growth, but uncommon in the typically poor tropical soil. Peoples in the area mixed the biochar into the ground and added waste, food refuse like bones, and other organic material. For reasons not fully understood, soil-friendly microbes thrived within the carbon-rich ground, adding to its overall health.

The result was *terra preta*, or black earth. Dark, fragrant, spongy, able to retain water and nutrients, deeper than six feet in some places, *terra preta* formed a super-fertile topsoil rich in carbon (hence the color). Petersen found a man who had farmed *terra preta* soil without fertilizer for an amaz-

ing four decades. Today, Brazilians harvest *terra preta* in the Amazon Basin and sell it to gardeners.

Using biochar to make new *terra preta* may allow farmers to restore depleted land. But the applications may also extend to helping the atmosphere. Johannes Lehmann, a soil scientist at Cornell University, has advocated that the slash-and-char method of clearing forest—burning trees at low temperatures, as Amazonian peoples did, to make biochar—replace the more harmful slash-and-burn method that pumps the carbon in the trees into the atmosphere as carbon dioxide, a greenhouse gas.

"By sequestering huge amounts of carbon," he said, "this technique constitutes a much longer and significant sink for atmospheric carbon dioxide than most other sequestration options, making it a powerful tool for long-term mitigation of climate change. In fact we have calculated that up to 12 percent of the carbon emissions produced by human activity could be offset annually if slash-and-burn were replaced by slash-and-char."

Others have worked on turning unwanted agricultural scraps like peanut shells and corn stalks into biochar in order to return the nutrients in those waste products to the soil. Eprida, a company in Athens, Georgia, develops machinery for the purpose of turning farm waste into biofuels and biochar. Whereas biofuels strive to be carbon neutral—balancing the release of carbon dioxide by burning the fuel with holding carbon dioxide in crops—the Eprida method, Lehmann said, was actually carbon negative. That is, it subtracts a net amount of carbon from the atmosphere by plowing it back into the soil, where it then feeds plant life that in turn traps more carbon dioxide.

Whether or not biochar becomes a solution depends on many things, first and foremost its effect on profits. It's also unclear if biochar and no-till can work together. Biochar's fine texture makes it vulnerable to wind, so mixing it into the dirt via tilling would be necessary.

Whereas the loss of trees in the Amazon is adding to the atmosphere's greenhouse gases, governments in other parts of the world are looking at planting trees as a defense against desertification. So-called greenbelts are hardly a new idea. In 1915, Morocco began planting greenbelts—a forerunner of the Dust Bowl shelterbelts—to protect fertile oasis areas and prevent blinding sandstorms on roads. The greenbelt idea gained a following in the 1960s as an answer not just to erosion but to a shortage of firewood. Algeria launched an ambitious plan to plant trees twenty kilometers deep along a line stretching 1,500 kilometers from east to west. That

proved unworkable, but the country has since added new dimensions to the original project, including the organization of tree plantations, planting fruit orchards to give local farmers income, and mixing forested areas with fields of cash crops and livestock fodder.

In the Sahel and Sahara, an alliance of nations has adopted the Great Green Wall Initiative. Conceived as a multi-level approach, the Great Green Wall Initiative is aimed not just at desertification but at poverty. The initiative, despite its lofty name, suggests turning away from gigantic programs like Algeria's, and instead concentrating on greening a portion of

at-risk areas while letting locals become "owners" with a personal interest in seeing the greenbelt succeed. This includes getting people involved in the planning stages and providing them with steady employment maintaining the trees.

In Asia, meanwhile, the Chinese government has initiated one of the largest ecological undertakings in human history. It's the Green Wall, a seventy-year, multibillion dollar effort to plant forest and shrubbery around the Gobi Desert. On the Loess Plateau, meanwhile, the Sloping Land Conservation Project pays local farmers to plant trees on hillsides or allow land to become grassland again. China's plans also include planting ground-cover plants able to grow in sandy soil.

Whether or not the Green Wall will work, however, is another matter. Overgrazing, farming on hillsides, and overpopulation have caused much of the soil depletion and desertification, and critics claim the Chinese government has yet to address any of these problems.

Inefficiency caused by China's top-down government system creates trouble, as well. A government plan may state the number of trees to be planted, for example, but often fails to specify the kinds of trees. As a result, the species going

onto the hillsides often will not grow in the soil. Local offi-
cials and farmers, the latter sometimes forced to plant trees
against their wishes, put in saplings to fill that year's quota
and then watch them die.

Experts see replanting Haiti's forests as an essential part
of dealing with that country's catastrophic erosion problem.
To fight the problem effectively, Haiti must address immense
social problems. Two-thirds of its people are unemployed.
Four out of five live in poverty and the country is consid-
ered the poorest in the Western Hemisphere. The continued
migration to the cities in search of a better life has led to
overcrowding and related increases in disease, hunger, crime,
and unsanitary conditions. On top of everything else, the
government is unstable and ineffective.

Everyone agrees that it's vital to get Haitians to participate.
The fate of millions of donated trees chopped down for charcoal illustrates what happens otherwise. One possible piece
of the solution is to encourage Haitians, like people in the
Sahel, to profit from the presence of healthy, plentiful trees.

The Organization for the Rehabilitation of the Environment
(ORE), a nonprofit group based in Miami, tries to convince
the farmers that caring for trees can be a job. ORE's donated
fruit trees and grafting material produce high-quality man-
goes for export. A good tree can provide income compara-
ble to selling the tree for wood. Furthermore, there's a new
mango crop every year, whereas dealing wood or charcoal
is a one-time sale.

Another project, funded by Snavely Forest Products of
Pittsburgh, sent a thousand trees to the country in hopes
that one of three new species—including the Paulownia, a
wide-leafed Asian tree able to grow up to fifteen feet in a

year—would take to the soil. If the project works, the new trees could provide a family with money in the form of lumber in five-to-seven years.

Organized efforts dedicated to re-greening Iceland go back to the 1880s. The country is home to more than fifty forestry clubs. In the late 1990s, the town of Mosfellsbae, located north of Reykjavik, enlisted students and scouting groups to plant trees on landfills and marginal land. Fences have gone up to discourage hungry sheep. Some farmers have taken financial aid to plant fruit groves and the government has encouraged a small industry that grows Christmas trees.

Iceland's reforestation efforts, however, are hampered by the climate. The sub-arctic's short growing season only allows slow growth; frequent late frosts wipe out saplings. To compensate, Icelanders have imported cold-weather species like the Siberian larch and Sitka spruce, with modest success.

Planting ground cover is another priority. The Alaskan lupine, another import, is a popular soil anchor. Hardy and used to high latitudes, the purple flower grows well in Iceland, even in some sandy regions, and the dead plant matter it provides reintroduces valuable organic matter to the soil. And

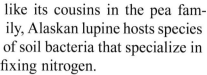

like its cousins in the pea family, Alaskan lupine hosts species of soil bacteria that specialize in fixing nitrogen.

But it's also gotten out of control. In areas fenced off from sheep, for example, the Alaskan lupine takes over the landscape before native Icelandic species can get established. The plant also steals sunlight from ground-hugging lichens and mosses. While beneficial in many ways, the Alaskan lupine offers an example of how balancing different ecological concerns—in this case erosion versus loss of biodiversity—complicates solutions to any soil depletion problem.

Whatever the future holds, and regardless of the answers provided by science and farmers, and from the experience acquired after millennia of farming, the time is coming when decisions will have to be made—on how we use fertilizer and fresh water, on how we use techniques like irrigation and plowing, and on how we approach climate change. Our wisdom regarding the ancient art of agriculture—or our lack of wisdom—will determine the fate of the soil we stand upon, and the fate of millions.

Guano: An All-Natural Fertilizer

Since pre-Columbian times, peoples in Peru have used bird droppings to fertilize their crops. They gave the product the name guano.

Guano accumulated over the ages on islands frequented by seabirds. Deposits on the Chincha Islands near Peru, one of the world's most famous sources, were two-hundred-feet deep. Guano is packed with three elements vital to fertile soils—it is 6 percent phosphorus, 9 percent nitrogen, and 2 percent potassium. In the era before artificial fertilizers, it was one of the best tools for improving soils.

As such, it was in tremendous demand, and hugely profitable. For part of the nineteenth century, guano provided Peru with most of its money from exports. Bolivia and Chile fought a war over access to guano islands that cost Bolivia its access to the Pacific Ocean. President Franklin Pierce, meanwhile, kicked off an odd land rush in 1856 when he signed the Guano Island Act, a law that authorized U.S. citizens to seize guano-rich islands to mine the droppings. Navassa Island near Haiti, previously a hideout for pirates, was one such claim. Baltimore's Navassa Phosphate Company mined it for most of the late 1800s.

The South Pacific also yielded guano profits. Germany took over Nauru, an egg-shaped island of just twenty-one square miles, to control its guano reserves, but mining really took off after World War I, when Britain confiscated the deposits over the islanders' complaints. Soon British, Australian, and New Zealand were sharing the profits of shipping a million tons of bird droppings per year off the island.

Guano mining on Nauru, like that for gold or coal else-where, led to environmental and financial devastation. Even as Nauru declared independence in 1968, the deposits were running out, and the island, its one major product all but mined out, sank into economic crisis. In 2000, large-scale mining ceased. Nauru's 10,000 people turned to aid from abroad for food. Donated airplane flights provided their sole connection to the rest of the world.

In recent years, the price of petroleum-based artificial fertilizers and the popularity of organic farming have renewed interest in guano. Locals with pickaxes and shovels have returned to Peru's guano islands to dig up the modest reserves left there. Guano in Peru goes for about $250 per ton. In more advanced countries, however, it can go for twice that price because of organic farmers' need for all-natural fertilizers.

The guano industry's modest revival is nothing compared to what happened in the 1800s. Nor is it going to be. Guano deposits take a long time to renew. And it happens even more slowly today, since the bird populations visiting the islands are a fraction of those in the past. Though Peru is shipping it again, and though small-scale mining has started again on Nauru, the world's guano is not expected to last. ■

Sources

Chapter One: Lessons of the Past

p. 11,   "Climate change and . . ." Lydia Polgreen, "A godsend for Darfur, or a curse?" *New York Times*, July 22, 2007.

p. 17,   "We overcrowd the world . . ." David R. Montgomery, *Dirt: The Erosion of Civilizations* (Berkeley, CA: University of California Press, 2007), 65.

p. 25,   "When you're living . . ." Richard Harris, "Viking farms tell cautionary tale," *NPR.com*, Dec. 3, 2007, http://www.npr.org/templates/story/story.php?storyId=16835101.

Chapter Two: Erosion

p. 39,   "We're not fools . . ." Tim Collie, "'We know that this is destroying the land, but charcoal keeps us alive.'" *South Florida Sun-Sentinel*, Dec. 7, 2003, http://www.sun-sentinel.com/news/sfl-haiti2dec07,0,7556000.story.

Chapter Three: Exhaustion

p. 51,   "Any attempt to explain . . ." Caroline Henderson, *Letters from the Dust Bowl*, (Norman, OK: University of Oklahoma Press, 2001), 140-141.

p. 53-54, "We Americans have been . . ." *American Experience: Surviving the Dust Bowl*, http://www.pbs.org/wgbh/amex/dust bowl/film more/transcript/index.html.

p. 70,   "It's like icing . . ." Joel K. Bourne, Jr., "A city's faulty armor," *National Geographic*, August 2007, http://ngm.nation algeographic.com/2007/08/new-orleans/online-extra-text/2.

Chapter Four: Desertification

p. 72, "Desertification exacerbates poverty . . ." U.N. Convention to
Combat Desertification, Desertification, global change,
and sustainable development," UNCCD Fact Sheet.
No. 10, Jan. 24, 2008, http://www.unccd.int/publicinfo/
factsheets/showfs.php?number=10.

p. 80, "Our model projects . . ." I.M. Held, T.L. Delworth, et. al,
"Simulation of Sahel drought in the 20th and 21st centuries,"
Proceedings of the National Academy of Sciences, Oct. 17, 2005,
http://www.pnas.org/content/102/50/17891.

Chapter Five: Rebuilding the Soil

p. 83, "Growing large amounts . . ." Leslie Berliant, "Dishing dirt with
David Montgomery," *Celsias*, Feb. 14, 2008, http://www.celsias.
com/article/dishing-dirt-with-david-montgomery/.

p. 89, "By sequestering huge amounts . . ." Susan L. Lang, "Cornell bio
geochemist shows how reproducing the Amazon's black soil
could increase fertility and reduce global warming,"
Cornell Chronicle, Feb. 18, 2006, http://www.news.cornell.edu/
stories/Feb06/AAAS.terra.preta.ssl.html

Bibliography

Books

Baskin, Yvonne, *The Work of Nature*. Washington, D.C.: Island Press, 1997.

Cannon, Terry, and Alan Jenkins, *The Geography of Contemporary China*. New York: Routledge, 1990.

De Villiers, Marq, and Sheila Hirtle, *Sahara: A Natural History*. New York: Walker and Company, 2002.

Diamond, Jared, *Collapse: How Societies Choose or Fail to Succeed*. New York: Penguin, 2005.

Egan, Timothy, *The Worst Hard Time: The Untold Story of Those Who Survived the Great American Dust Bowl*. Boston: Houghton Mifflin, 2005.

European Environment Agency, *Impacts of Europe's Changing Climate: 2008 Indicator-based Assessment* (EEA Report No. 4/2008). Luxembourg: Office for Official Publications of the European Communities, 2008.

Faulkner, Edward H., *Plowman's Folly*. Washington, D.C.: Island Press, 1988.

Henderson, Caroline, *Letters from the Dust Bowl*. Norman, OK: University of Oklahoma Press, 2001.

Lehmann, Johannes, Dirse C. Kirn, Bruno Glaser, and William I. Woods (eds.), *Amazonian Black Earths*. Amsterdam: Kluwer Academic Publishers, 2004.

Lincoln, W. Bruce, *The Conquest of a Continent: Siberia and the Russians*. Ithaca, NY: Cornell University Press, 2007.

Logan, William Bryant, *Dirt: The Elastic Skin of the Earth*. New York: W.W. Norton, 2006. Mann, Charles, *1491: New Revelations of the Americas Before Columbus*. New York: Knopf, 2005.

Manning, Richard. *Grassland: The History, Biology, Politics and Promise of the American Prairie*. New York: Penguin, 1997.

Meine, Curt. *Aldo Leopold: His Life and Work*. Madison, WI: University of Wisconsin Press, 1991.

Montgomery, David R.. *Dirt: The Erosion of Civilizations*. Berkeley, CA: University of California Press, 2007.

Josephson, Paul R. *Industrialized Nature: Brute Force Technology and the Transformation of the Natural World*. Washington, D.C.: Island Press, 2002.

Novacek, Terra. *Our 100-Million-Year-Old Ecosystem and the Threats That Now Put It at Risk*. New York: Farrar, Straus and Giroux, 2007.

Sahara and Sahel Observatory. *The Great Green Wall Initiative of the Sahara and Sahel*. Tunis, Tunisia: Sahara and Sahel Observatory (OSS), 2008.

Schele, Linda and David Freidel. *A Forest of Kings: The Untold Story of the Ancient Maya*. New York: William Morrow and Co., 1990.

Shiva, Vandana. *Stolen Harvest: The Hijacking of the Global Food Supply*. Cambridge, MA: South End Press, 2000.

Waldbauer, Gilbert. *What Good Are Bugs?* Cambridge, MA: Harvard University Press, 2003.

Wilson, E.O. *The Future of Life*. New York: Knopf, 2002.

Periodicals

Bourne, Jr., Joel K. "A city's faulty armor." *National Geographic*, August, 2007
http://ngm.nationalgeographic.com/2007/08/new-orleans/online-extra-text/2.

"Dirt poor." *National Geographic*, Sept. 2008, vol. 214, no. 3.

Diamond, Jared. "Easter Island revisited." Science, Sept. 21, 2007, vol. 317. no. 5845.

Gans, Jason, Murray Wolinsky, and John Dunbar. "Computational Improvements
Reveal Great Bacterial Diversity and High Metal Toxicity in Soil." Science,
Aug. 26, 2005, Vol. 309., no. 5739.

Hunt, Terry, L. "Rethinking Easter Island's ecological catastrophe." *Journal of
Archaeological Science*, 2007, vol. 34.

Mann, Charles. "The good earth." *National Geographic*, Sept. 2008, vol. 214, no. 3.

———. "The real dirt on rainforest fertility." Science, Aug. 9, 2002: vol. 297. no. 5583.

Marris, Emma. "Black is the new green." *Nature*, Aug. 2006, vol. 442, no. 10.

Ratliff, Evan. "The great green wall of China." *Wired*, April 2003, vol. 11, no. 4.

Ryle, John. "Disaster in Darfur." *New York Review of Books*, Aug. 12, 2004, vol. 51, no. 13.

Online

Achenbach, Joel. "A dead zone in the Gulf of Mexico." *Washington Post*, July 31, 2008.
http://www.washingtonpost.com/wp-
dyn/content/story/2008/07/31/ST2008073100349.html.

Alleyn, Patrick. "The Chinese Dust Bowl." *Walrus*, Oct. 2007.
http://www.walrusmagazine.com/articles/2007.10-china-desert.

Aquin, Benoit. "China Dust Bowl." *Time*.
http://www.time.com/time/photogallery/0,29307,1738165,00.html.

Bennett, Drake. "The future of dirt." *Boston Globe*, April 27, 2008.
http://www.boston.com/bostonglobe/ideas/articles/2008/04/27/the_future_of_dirt/.

Berliant, Leslie. "Dishing dirt with David Montgomery." *Celsias*, Feb. 14, 2008.
http://www.celsias.com/article/dishing-dirt-with-david-montgomery/.

Biello, David. "Grounds for hope." *Scientific American*, June 8, 2006.
http://www.sciam.com/article.cfm?id=grounds-for-hope.

Borenstein, Seth. "Good soil critical in food crisis." Associated Press, May 8, 2008.
http://dsc.discovery.com/news/2008/05/08/soil-food-crisis.html.

Brahic, Catherine. "Amazon hides an ancient urban landscape."
New Scientist, Aug. 29, 2008.
http://www.newscientist.com/article/dn14624-amazon-hides-an-ancient-urban-
landscape.html?feedId=online-news_rss20.

Branigan, Tania. "Soil erosion threatens land of 100 million Chinese, survey finds."
Guardian, Nov. 21, 2008.
http://www.guardian.co.uk/world/2008/nov/21/china-soil-erosion-population.

British Broadcasting Corporation. "Oceans linked to Sahel drought." *BBC Online*, Oct.
14, 2003.
http://news.bbc.co.uk/1/hi/sci/tech/3191174.stm.

Brown, Lester R. "Around the globe, farmers losing ground." Inter-Press Service, June
27, 2007.
http://ipsnews.net/news.asp?idnews=38343.

———."Replanting the planet." Inter-Press Service, July 10, 2007.
http://ipsnews.net/news.asp?idnews=38486.

Casselman, Anne. "Inspired by Ancient Amazonians, a Plan to Convert Trash into Environmental Treasure." Scientific American, May 15, 2007. http://www.sciam.com/article.cfm?id=pyrolyisis-terra-preta-could-eliminate-garbage-generate-oil-carbon-sequestration.

Collie, Tim. "Haiti: 'The world doesn't have any idea how bad this situation is getting." South Florida Sun-Sentinel, Dec. 7, 2003. http://www.sun-sentinel.com/news/sfl-haiti1dec07,0,7162783.story.

"It's an unnatural disaster, a man-made disaster." South Florida Sun-Sentinel, Dec. 7,\2003. http://www.sun-sentinel.com/news/sfl-haiti6dec07,0,1128875.story.

"'We know that this is destroying the land, but charcoal keeps us alive.'" South Florida Sun-Sentinel, Dec. 7, 2003. http://www.sun-sentinel.com/news/sfl-haiti2dec07,0,7556000.story.

Commonwealth of Australia. "Australia's Salinity Problem." http://www.napswq.gov.au/publications/brochures/pubs/salinity.pdf.

"Caring For Our Country." March 2008. http://www.nrm.gov.au/publications/factsheets/pubs/cfoc-general.pdf.

"Caring For Our Country: Outcomes, 2008-2013." 2008. http://www.nrm.gov.au/publications/books/pubs/caring-outcomes.pdf.

Connor, Steve. "Soil crisis is holding back African recovery." The Independent, March 31, 2006. http://www.independent.co.uk/news/world/africa/soil-crisis-is-holding-back-african-recovery-472161.html.

Copley, John. "Millions of bacteria species revealed underfoot." New Scientist, Aug. 25, 2005. http://www.newscientist.com/article.ns?id=dn7904

Dangerfield, Whitney. "The mystery of Easter Island." Smithsonian, April 1, 2007. http://www.smithsonianmag.com/people-places/The_Mystery_of_Easter_Island.html.

Davidson, Phil. "Flood kills 2000 as Haiti faces a year of disaster." The Independent, Sept. 24, 2004. http://www.independent.co.uk/news/world/americas/floods-kill-2000-as-haiti-faces-a-year-of-disaster-547441.html.

Dealey, Sam. "No moral clarity in Darfur." Time, March 6, 2008. http://www.time.com/time/magazine/article/0,9171,1720105,00.html

Delfavero, Gina. "Economics drive many farmers to no-till planting." Pittsburgh Tribune-Review, Jan. 20, 2006. http://www.pittsburghlive.com/x/pittsburghtrib/s_415344.html.

Eswaran, H., R. Lal, and P.F. Reich. "Land degradation: an overview." Responses to Land Degradation, New Delhi: Oxford, 2001. http://soils.usda.gov/use/worldsoils/papers/land-degradation-overview.html.

Faris, Stephan. "The real roots of Darfur." Atlantic Monthly, April 2007. http://www.theatlantic.com/doc/200704/darfur-climate.

"Haiti at crossroads." Food and Agriculture Organization of the United Nations, Dec. 18, 2006. http://www.fao.org/Newsroom/en/news/2006/1000463/index.html.

Harris, Richard. "Iceland seeks to restore soils." National Public Radio, Dec. 22, 2007. http://www.npr.org/templates/story/story.php?storyId=17548004.

"In Iceland, unintended witnesses to climate change." National Public Radio, Dec. 4, 2007. http://www.npr.org/templates/story/story.php?storyId=16859927

"Viking farms tell cautionary tale." National Public Radio, Dec. 3, 2007. http://www.npr.org/templates/story/story.php?storyId=16835101

Held, I.M., T.L. Delworth, et. al. "Simulation of Sahel drought in the 20th and 21st centuries." Proceedings of the National Academy of Sciences, Oct. 17, 2005. http://www.pnas.org/content/102/50/17891.

Helmore, Ed. "How Haiti hopes to break the cycle of disaster: restoring its lost forests." Guardian, Nov. 23, 2008. http://www.guardian.co.uk/environment/2008/nov/23/forests-flooding.

Heuck, Doug. "Haiti: In search of hope." *Pittsburgh Quarterly*, Spring-Summer 2006. http://www.pittsburghquarterly.com/pages/spring_summer2006/ss2006_26haiti.htm.

Jones, Tamsyn. "The scoop on dirt." *E Magazine*, Sept.-Oct. 2006. http://www.emagazine.com/view/?3344.

Jowit, Juliette. "Drought land 'will be abandoned.'" *Guardian*, Nov. 2, 2008. http://www.guardian.co.uk/environment/2008/nov/02/climate-change-desertification-water-drought

Kissane, Michael J. "Seeing the forest for the trees: land reclamation in Iceland." *Scandinavian Review*, Spring 1998. http://findarticles.com/p/articles/mi_qa3760/is_199804/ai_n8798492/pg_1?tag=artBody;col1.

LaFranchi, Howard. "Haiti's elusive search for unity." *Christian Science Monitor*, March 11, 2004. http://www.csmonitor.com/2004/0311/p06s01-woam.html#anchor1.

Lagan, Bernard. "Drought turns fertile heart into dustbowl." *Times Online*, Jan. 4, 2008. http://www.timesonline.co.uk/tol/news/environment/article3129020.ece.

Lang, Susan L. "Cornell biogeochemist shows how reproducing the Amazon's black soil could increase fertility and reduce global warming." *Cornell Chronicle*, Feb. 18, 2006. http://www.news.cornell.edu/stories/Feb06/AAAS.terra.preta.ssl.html.

Langewiesche, William. "The world in its extreme." *Atlantic Monthly*, Nov. 1991. http://www.theatlantic.com/unbound/langew/extreme.htm.

Latiak, Ted. "Corps says levees not ready for Katrina's waves, soil erosion leading culprit." *Popular Mechanics*, June 1, 2006. http://www.popularmechanics.com/blogs/science_news/2911566.html.

Lipper, Leslie. "Dirt Poor: Poverty, Farmers, and Soil Resource Investment." *Two Essays on Socio-economic Aspects of Soil Degradation*. Rome: Food and Agricultural Organization of the United Nations, 2003. http://www.fao.org/t77777ykjhjk9docrep/004/y1796e/y1796e02.htm#TopOfPage.

Lowman, Meg. "Iceland is a country of extreme environments and extreme energy." *International Herald-Tribune*, July 17, 2005. http://www.heraldtribune.com/article/20050717/COLUMNIST18/507170799.

Macartney, Jane. "Great green wall of China fails to keep out dust." *Times Online*, May 10, 2005. http://www.timesonline.co.uk/tol/news/world/article520652.ece.

Maksimov, Boris. "Rolling back Iceland's big desert." *BBC Online*, Feb. 8, 2005. http://news.bbc.co.uk/1/hi/sci/tech/4737743.stm.

McIntosh, Phyllis. "Desertification: Earth's silent scourge." U.S. State Department, Sept. 13, 2004. http://usinfo.state.gov/products/pubs/desertific/.

McLaughlin, Abraham, and Christian Allen Purefoy. "Hunger is spreading in Africa." *Christian Science Monitor*, Aug. 1, 2005. http://www.csmonitor.com/2005/0801/p01s02-woaf.html.

Mitchell, Garry. "'Living shorelines' eyed to stop coastal erosion." Associated Press, Oct. 25, 2008. http://www.denverpost.com/nationworld/ci_10814613.

Montgomery, David R. "A case for no-till farming." *Scientific American*, June 30, 2008. http://www.pittsburghlive.com/x/pittsburghtrib/s_415344.html.

Muckel, Gary B. *Understanding Soil Risks and Hazards*. Washington, D.C.: U.S. Department of Agriculture, 2004. ftp://ftp-fc.sc.egov.usda.gov/NSSC/Soil_Risks/risk_low_res.pdf.

Owens, David W., Peter Jopke, et. al. "Soil Erosion from Two Small Construction Sites, Dane County, Wisconsin." U.S. Geological Survey Fact Sheet FS-109-00, Aug. 2000. http://wi.water.usgs.gov/pubs/fs-109-00/.

Paulson, Tom. "The lowdown on topsoil: It's disappearing." *Seattle Post-Intelligencer*, Jan. 22, 2008. http://seattlepi.nwsource.com/local/348200_dirt22.html.

Pearce, Fred. "A sea change in the Sahel." *New Scientist*, Feb. 2, 1991. http://www.newscientist.com/article/mg12917542.600-a-sea-change-in-the-sahel-climate-researchers-can-nowpredict-african-drought-in-most-years-but-that-doesnt-mean-they-know-whyit-is-happening-.html.

Pieri, Christian, Guy Evers, John Landers, and Paul O'Connell. "A road map to conventional no-till farming." Agriculture and Rural Development working paper, International Bank for Reconstruction and Development, 2002. http://www-wds.worldbank.org/external/default/WDSContentServer/WDSP/IB/2002/08/29/000094946_02080704010441/Rendered/PDF/multi0page.pdf.

Polgreen, Lydia. "A godsend for Darfur, or a curse?" *New York Times*, July 22, 2007. http://www.nytimes.com/2007/07/22/weekinreview/22polgreen.html.

Power, Samantha. "Dying in Darfur." *New Yorker*, Aug. 30, 2004. http://www.newyorker.com/archive/2004/08/30/040830fa_fact1.

Radford, Tim. "Loss of soil carbon 'will speed global warming.'" *Guardian*, Sept. 8, 2005. http://www.guardian.co.uk/science/2005/sep/08/sciencenews.research1.
——— "Soil erosion as big a problem as global warming, say scientists." *Guardian*, Feb. 14, 2004. http://www.guardian.co.uk/world/2004/feb/14/science.environment.

Ravilious, Kate, "Food crisis feared as fertile land runs out." *Guardian*, Dec. 6, 2005. http://www.guardian.co.uk/science/2005/dec/06/agriculture.food.

Reganold, John P., and David R. Huggins. "No-till: How farmers are saving the soil by parking their plows." *Scientific American*, June 30, 2008. http://www.sciam.com/article.cfm?id=no-till.

Roach, John. "Superdirt made lost Amazon cities possible?" *National Geographic News*, Nov. 19, 2008. http://news.nationalgeographic.com/news/2008/11/081119-lost-cities-amazon.html.

Romero, Simon, "Peru guards its guano as demand soars again." *New York Times*, May 30, 2008. http://www.nytimes.com/2008/05/30/world/americas/30peru.html?_r=2&pagewanted=1.

Sample, Ian. "Global food crisis looms as climate change and population growth strip fertile land." *Guardian*, August 31, 2007. http://www.guardian.co.uk/environment/2007/aug/31/climatechange.food.

Scheyer, J.M., and K.W. Hipple. *Urban Soil Primer*. Lincoln, NE: United States Department of Agriculture, 2005. http://soils.usda.gov/use/urban/downloads/primer(screen).pdf

Schwartz, John. "Critic says levee repairs show signs of flaws." *New York Times*, May 7, 2007. http://www.nytimes.com/2007/05/07/us/07levees.html.

Serchuk, David. "The big dry." *Forbes*, June 19, 2008. http://www.forbes.com/2008/06/19/australia-drought-restrictions-tech-water08-cx_ds_0619dry.html.

Sidney, Daniel. "The big dry." *Time*, May 22, 2008. http://www.time.com/time/magazine/article/0,9171,1808502,00.html.

Swaminathan, Nikhil. "Dust Bowl 2.0: Is the southwest drying up?" *Scientific American*, April 5, 2007. http://www.sciam.com/article.cfm?id=southwest-america-drying-climate

Tayler, Letta. "Fruit of their labor." *Hartford Courant*, Jan. 3, 2006. courant.com/business/ny-woside034573598jan03,0,4958811.story.

Tenenbaum, David. "Traditional drought and uncommon famine in the Sahel." *Whole Earth Review*, Summer 1986. http://findarticles.com/p/articles/mi_m1510/is_1986_Summer/ai_4284343/pg_1?tag=artBody;col1.

Tennesen, Michael. "Black gold of the Amazon." *Discover*, April 30, 2007. http://discovermagazine.com/2007/apr/black-gold-of-the-amazon/

article_view?b_start:int=3&-C=.

Tucker, William. "The next American Dust Bowl—and how to avert it." *Atlantic Monthly*, July 1979. http://www.theatlantic.com/doc/197907/ sustainable-agriculture. United Nations, *Learning to Combat Desertification* (teaching kit). http://unesdoc.unesco.org/images/0012/001258/125816e.pdf.

U.N. Department of Economic and Social Affairs. *Trends in Sustainable Development.* New York: United Nations, 2008. http://www.un.org/esa/sustdev/publications/trends2008/fullreport.pdf

U.N. Office for the Coordination of Human Affairs, "Mali: All it takes to save the lakes from climate change is money." *IRIN*, June 5, 2008. http://www.irinnews.org/report.aspx?ReportID=78604.

U.S. Agency for International Development. "Haiti: Environmental degradation slowed." http://www.usaid.gov/pubs/cbj2002/lac/ht/521-002.html.

U.S. Department of Agriculture. "Erosion and sentimentation on construction sites." Soil Quality-Urban Technical Note No. 1 ftp://ftp-fc.sc.egov.usda.gov/IL/urbanmnl/appendix/u01.pdf

Vidal, John. "Desert cities are living on borrowed time, UN warns." *Guardian*, June 5, 2006. http://www.guardian.co.uk/environment/2006/jun/05/climatechange. climatechange.

Walsh, Bryan. "The Gulf's growing dead zone." *Time*, June 17, 2008. http://www.time.com/time/nation/article/0,8599,1815305,00.html.

Wilentz, Amy. "Hurricanes and Haiti." *Los Angeles Times*, Sept. 13, 2008. http://www.latimes.com/news/opinion/sunday/commentary/la-oe-wilentz13-2008sep13,0,5320045.story.

Williams, Carol J. "Haiti can't gain ground on erosion." *Los Angeles Times*, Nov. 17, 2003. http://articles.latimes.com/2003/nov/17/world/fg-erosion17

Wilson, Conrad. "Is corn boom expanding Gulf of Mexico 'dead zone?'" *Minneapolis Star-Tribune*, June 2, 2008. http://www.startribune.com/local/19473599.html?location_refer=Homepage.

Xie Yu, "Land erosion 'threat to food supply.'" *China Daily*, Nov. 22, 2008. http://www.chinadaily.com.cn/bizchina/2008-11/22/content_7230508.htm.

Young, Emma. "Easter Island: A monumental collapse?" *New Scientist*, July 31, 2006. http://www.newscientist.com/channel/being-human/mg19125621.100-easter-island-a-monumental-collapse.html.

Youth, Howard. "Saving the Sahel." *ZooGoer*, May-June 2002. http://nationalzoo.si.edu/Publications/ZooGoer/2002/3/savingsahel.cfm.

Web Sites

Australian Government: Caring for our Country
http://www.nrm.gov.au/

**International Development Association and the World Bank:
The Loess Plateau**
http://go.worldbank.org/RGXNXF4A00

Kansas State University: Dust Bowl photo archive
http://www.weru.ksu.edu/new_weru/multimedia/dustbowl/dustbowlpics.html

Sahara and Sahel Observatory
http://www.oss-online.org/

United Nations Convention to Combat Desertification
http://www.unccd.int/

U.S. Department of Agriculture: Global Desertification Vulnerability Map
http://soils.usda.gov/use/worldsoils/mapindex/desert.html

U.S. Department of Agriculture: Water Erosion Vulnerability Map
http://soils.usda.gov/use/worldsoils/mapindex/erosh2o.html

Photo Credits

Photographs in this book are reproduced by permission of **Alamy**: 12 &
13 (blickwinkel/Alamy); 32 & 33 (Dennis Cox/Alamy); 34 & 35 (Keren
Su/China Span/Alamy); 42 & 43 (Eye Ubiquitous/Alamy); 55 (Photo
Researchers/Alamy); 69 (Marvin Dembinsky Photo Associates/Alamy);
70 (Denita Delimont/Alamy); 74 & 75 (Andrew Woodley/Alamy) 80
& 81 ; 82 (frans lemmens/Alamy); 97 (Mark Bowler/Alamy); 98 & 99
(Mary Evans Picture Library/Alamy); **Shutterstock, Inc.**: 6 & 7, 9, 10,
15 & 16, 18 & 19, 20 & 21, 24 & 25, 26 & 27, 28 & 29, 30, 40 & 41, 44
& 45, 46 & 47, 48, 57, 60 & 61, 62 & 63, 64, 66 & 67, 69, 70, 76, 78 & 79,
84 &85, 88, 89, 93 & 93, 94 & 95; **Private Collection**: 38 & 39, 51, 52 &
53, 76, 92.

Index